Climbing
the
Success
L

DDER

Other Books by Virgie M. Binford

Are You Famous?
I Want to Be Just Like You!

Avenues for Success:
Turning Adversity into Opportunity through
Strong Support Systems

Character Education:
The Birth of Hope through Unconditional Love
for Total Fulfillment
(with Rona Leach)

Self-Esteem Enhancers:
Inner-Directed Guidelines for Successful Living
(with Dorothy N. Cowling)

Climbing
the
Success
L▲DDER

The Ten Commandments
of Effective Parent
Education Performance

Virgie M. Binford

Second Edition

Providence House Publishers
PROVIDENCE PUBLISHING CORPORATION
FRANKLIN, TENNESSEE

Printed in the United States of America

10   09   08   07   06   1   2   3   4   5

Library of Congress Control Number: 2006900192

ISBN-13: 978-1-57736-362-0
ISBN-10: 1-57736-362-0

Cover design by Joey McNair

PROVIDENCE HOUSE PUBLISHERS
an imprint of
Providence Publishing Corporation
238 Seaboard Lane • Franklin, Tennessee 37067
www.providence-publishing.com
800-321-5692

*With love and messages of positive thinking
to Kimberly Monette Redd
and
Percy Woodrow Redd III,
my wonderful grandchildren, whom I honor.*

—Contents—

Contents

—Preface—

The seeds for the contents of this book were planted in early childhood when my best teacher—my grandmother—used to sing:

We are climbing Jacob's ladder,
We are climbing Jacob's ladder,
We are climbing Jacob's ladder,
Soldiers of the Cross.

Every rung goes higher—higher,
Every rung goes higher—higher,
Every rung goes higher—higher,
Soldiers of the Cross.

Although I lived in an economically deprived environment, I grew up as a wealthy, positive thinker. The message of hope, faith, and love catapulted me beyond my physical surroundings to a promised land of beauty of the soul, mind, and spirit.

Commandments of mother wit coupled with those of the Holy Scriptures made me know that, as a "soldier of the Cross" of adversities, there was a ladder to climb. I could go up and over any obstacle that was a stumbling block to an open-ended land of opportunities.

If this vision of a new dawning of success could shine in my life from the messages of a loving grandmother, then there are messages of love; sincere, honest praise; and positive reinforcement for everyone. These messages of hope and aspiration can be translated into success in as many ways as there are interpretations of the word.

Since all of us on this planet earth are, in one way or another, climbing Jacob's ladder, we need positive messages and boosters to help us in our struggles upward. There is no better way to get them than from our first and most effective teachers—our parents and/or parenting-ones (those who serve in parental roles).

Thoughts and experiences shared in this volume will, I hope, be guiding lights for those climbing ladders of success in many favorable ways.

—Acknowledgments—

A twenty-year span of time continues to reinforce my belief that the foundation of excellence in education begins in the home. That beginning is with parents and parenting-ones acting as primary caretakers of children.

Since 1985, I served as a facilitator of teaching and learning in various educational settings in my career and in my home and family interactions as a mother, grandmother, and great-grandmother. Added to these opportunities are the various settings as a volunteer in organizations and agencies serving children and youth. These activities provide me with additional chances to operate as a servant leader, finding needs and filling them.

Teamwork is a valuable ingredient for support and rein-forcement in climbing the success ladder in parent education/performance. My gratitude for generating interests and for sharing ideas, enthusiasm, and creative strategies is expressed to my professional advisor and publishing agent, Mary Bray Wheeler, from Providence Publishing Corporation. She has guided my growth and development as a writer and has continued genuine friendship in building my "I Can" attitude.

Special thanks and grateful appreciation are expressed to my coworker and friend, Debra Jones. She utilized her skills, working hours in preparation of a draft to make the revision of this book possible. Her expertise in helping me express my thoughts to my readers kept me on track. She helped make my ideas unquestion-able in their interpretation and aided in the application of suggested practices in child growth and development.

I wish to express my unconditional love for generations of families whose faith, hope, and love have been generously shared with me through the years. Their positive feedback on my contributions as a teacher and learner in home, school, and community are evident in this volume.

Mentorship played a valuable role in making me an inner-winner in various curricular and extracurricular activities. They are too numerous to name because of the distinct roles they played in helping me succeed in achieving my goals and objectives. Special gratitude is expressed to my teacher and genuine friend, Dr. Dorothy N. Cowling, who helped me turn obstacles in life into opportunities to achieve in spite of handicapping conditions. For all persons whose names I did not mention, please accept my appreciation for your constant support.

Climbing
the
Success
LADDER

A Child Speaks

*Love is teaching me that
the world is a better place.
By showing me through your actions
more learning will be caught than taught.*

—Prologue—

Parent Education:

Then and Now, A Review of the Past

Since creation of people on earth, the parent has served as teacher of children, sometimes in a hit-or-miss fashion. The Hebrew culture, documented in biblical history, is one example of how human cultures have evolved intact throughout generations through the use of informal systems of parent education.

Braun and Edwards reviewed the history of parent education, which historically has played an important part of teaching and learning. Survival skills such as fishing, hunting, cooking, harvesting, and personal grooming were taught to children by parents. Words, ideas, values, and skills were transmitted in an informal manner. Careers related to functioning as an effective parent didn't exist and the rule of thumb was to use mother wit to do what came naturally in parenting.[1]

Under this system of guidance, the growth and development of children were left with much assistance to be desired. Without parent education, it was difficult to know and respond to needs of children.

In this twenty-first century, we are aware that the profession of parents may be undertaken by any adult. Yet, parenting-ones—parents, grandparents, and guardians—know that parent education is needed to cope with the ever-increasing needs of children. In this computer age of challenges in our society, the task of being effective parents takes greater expertise.

Recognizing that formal schooling takes approximately one-third of a child's time, parents need to know and understand the importance of having knowledge, skills, and techniques of extending teaching and learning in the home.

Formal schooling is important, and every parent, in spite of how little or how much formal training he or she possesses, can become a parent educator who uses desirable teaching behaviors when interacting with children.

In today's world, problems encountered by children in many areas, such as overcrowded classrooms, mind-deteriorating drugs, and unemployment and underemployment in the family, are numerous. Changes in family structures, varied working schedules of parents, and increases in crime rates are signals of the need for closer parent-child relationships. Parents can help to erase these deterrents to self-fulfillment by providing a support system of positive reinforcement that helps each child climb the ladder of success physically, mentally, emotionally, and socially.

According to Callahan, parents must learn to parent effectively and must be conscious about this important job.[2] A primary task for parents in the process of education, according to Schiavone, is to have genuine respect for a child as a person and high expectations that he/she will do his/her best.[3]

Focusing on positive attributes of a child and minimizing negative traits will provide incentive for learning faster. Parents must see themselves as capable teachers of their own children, enriching and extending formal systems of education. As noted by Breivogel, Greenwood, and Sterling, parents must have the opportunity to participate in the educational decisions which affect their children.[4] They, then, must be assertive in assuming their responsibilities in guiding the growth and development of their offspring. When this happens, as affirmed by White and Watts, the most competent children are those whose mothers (or parenting-ones) provide positive reinforcement, teach children often, and provide a stimulating environment.[5]

In making a special observation encouraging more participation by parents in schooling, John W. Warner, United States Senator from Virginia, stated that "parents are the most important teachers a child will ever have."[6] This point of view was accentuated by researchers such as Ira Gordon, Nancy Rutenber, R. L. Weinberg, and L. G. Weinberg. They reported that not only are parents important as teachers, but they are also important as advocates for children.[7] Evidences of success in utilizing parents as teachers were revealed in six parent-education programs of research and implementation reported by Olmsted, Rubin, True, and Revicki in 1980. The roles of parents in these programs ranged from parents as teachers of infants to parents of school-age children. In both short-term and longitudinal studies, results of the research and implementation yielded positive affirmation favoring parents as teachers over comparison groups.

Based on the literature, parents as teachers of their own children represent important rungs on the ladder of success. However, it must not be assumed that parents are born with necessary skills for functioning as effective teachers of their children. What can be assumed is that parents desire the best for their children. They will accept and utilize commandments that will increase and enrich their performances in parent education.[8]

In assessing the contributions of public education in our society, Leinwand revealed that schools are but one agency for the education of the public. Based on his research he added that family and faith, library and museum, the workplace and the leisure place, visual and print media, and art and music each play a role in education.[9]

Ann Lloyd declared in *Tips and Tricks: Home Schooling Survival* that parents should let their children see them as learners. This will convince them that learning is a lifelong process.[10]

In *Making Schools Better*, Larry Martz shared research which proved that children do better if their parents take an active interest in their schooling, and teachers and principals repeat like a mantra, "Schools filled with parents are just better schools."[11]

Ronald K. Pierce, in his work *What Are We Trying to Teach Them Anyway? A Father's Focus on School Reform*, concluded that "an expanded role for schools must also provide a free market in varying programs of learning. Parents and children must be involved in choosing a program that suits their individual needs."[12]

In *Chicken Soup for the Parent's Soul*, Jack Canfield and associates shared an incredible view on various components of parent education and involvement in teaching and learning. They used a variety of approaches by guest writers who shared stories of survival, joys, sorrows, and strategies for overcoming obstacles of families during periods of growth and development of their children across generations. Their messages encompassed the values of teamwork, challenges, and joy in the powerful responsibilities in parenting and getting an education in the process.[13]

In retrospect, the perception of many teachers and learners concludes that parent education/involvement has always been a building block for success in life. Literacy in every generation has been regarded as an important requirement for making the survival of children possible in a competitive society.

Regardless of limited educational competencies of parents and other caretakers, they expressed desires to observe children and youth climbing the ladder of success.

The torch of support and positive reinforcement is a continuous responsibility of systems of education. Education needs to engage in a partnership that manifests the dreams of parenting-ones to make their goals for children a reality. Through teamwork of faith, hope, and unconditional love for all children, their wings of success will allow them to soar to immeasurable elevations.

*Messages of love given by caring,
concerned, and committed parents
will be passports to unlimited success.*

Messages from the Top of the Success Ladder by Recipients of Parental Support

In many cities, towns, and rural communities from Maine to Mexico, there are people who are successful in careers, family life, civics, business, health, social organizations, and places of worship. Their enthusiasm and zest for solving problems that affect self and others are contagious. However, there are those who grew up in similar economic, physical, and social conditions who flounder as they live unfulfilled lives in many areas. What made the difference between those who are feeling, acting, looking upward, and climbing ladders of success and those who are hovering at the bottom rungs of the ladder, criticizing, condemning, and complaining about their circumstances? In many instances, effective parents made the difference.

For more than fifty years I have experienced working with parent education/involvement programs. I have encountered numerous success stories of children who have succeeded despite external circumstances that favored failure. The help of a perceptive, loving, and supportive parent or parenting-one almost always resulted in overcoming adversities and realizing success. The following pages outline evidences of parents helping children climb ladders of success in ten reports of positive messages heard by their children.

As I promised the interviewees, I haven't mentioned their names. They will be listed as Messengers A through K, as they recall reasons for their success in some aspects of their lives.

MESSENGER A

This young adult is a practicing attorney and a partner in an educational consulting firm with her mother and two brothers.

A's father died when she and her brothers were very young. On a school teacher's salary and with limited financial resources, her mother made it possible for the children to get an education.

According to A, she and her brothers never knew there were limitations on what they could achieve. Not only did their mother encourage them by giving each child personal attention daily, but she was involved in their special activities. She structured family learning activities that did not require money.

> Not only did their mother encourage them by giving each child personal attention daily, but she was involved in their special activities.

Problems that might impede their progress in any given field, such as racism, sexism, poverty, etc., were never discussed. Instead, emphasis was placed on myriad opportunities for success. The family read about various careers together and talked about criteria for earning them.

A said that she had made her decision to become an attorney prior to becoming a teenager. Some of the games she and her brothers played at home were role-playing different careers. The one she liked best was acting roles of lawyers in different settings that included courtrooms, big corporations, and the Supreme Court. Their mother kept generating interest by asking questions, serving as a mediator, and praising whenever it was deserved.

MESSENGER B

An esteemed teacher, Messenger B is married and has one toddler. She said she heard positive messages from her father and mother as far back as she could remember and the messages were repeated over and over again. A typical comment was, "Be somebody and learn all you can."

As a laborer, her father worked hard. Yet he took an extra job on a part-time basis to provide money for weekend family outings, books, and music lessons for B.

Her mother worked part-time jobs that would allow for volunteer activities and permit her to be home when B got out of school. Recalling her early years in school, B said her mother always talked with her about her school activities. She would ask questions such as:

- What have you learned in school today?
- What was the most fun?
- What kind of work did you do?
- What do you need to do to prepare to have a good day in
- school tomorrow?
- Teach me the way your teacher taught you so I can have fun learning too.

According to B, playing teacher with her mother was fun. During dinner, B said she was the center of attention when her mother shared what good things she had learned from B that day. What information she omitted, B would eagerly supply.

She said her parents used every opportunity to share in her school activities. This ranged from serving as a room mother to involvement in parent-teacher meetings. They also attended school programs whenever B participated. Her father bragged about saving vacation days to attend school functions because he knew his child was going to be "a great lady."

These messages of high expectations motivated B to succeed. Having a head start playing the game of teacher with her mother created a desire to become an educator.

MESSENGER C

The youngest of five children, C said her father died when she was very young. Her widowed mother worked hard to support, encourage, and share time with each child. She sacrificed, bought a house, and involved the children in planting and taking care of a flower and vegetable garden. As a team, they made their environment beautiful and experienced joy in learning inside and outside of the home.

Not only did C's mother plan learning activities at home, but she found opportunities for them to participate in community programs such as scouting and church. Their mother's message, according to C, was "you can become anything you want to become if you try hard enough." This message, she said, was largely responsible for her success as an outstanding secretary and office manager, with a second career as a real estate agent. C models her mother's positive messages with quality time with her own two children. She engages in activities and helps them experience success in things they enjoy. She is proud of their progress. One is an honor student in college and the other is doing well in high school.

MESSENGER D

The oldest of twelve brothers and sisters, D stated that she did not realize that her family was economically deprived. Her father was a hard worker of two jobs and provided basic needs for them. Her mother was an energetic homemaker and creatively taught her children how to do many things early in life.

D said she was made to feel proud that, as a big sister, she could teach younger brothers and sisters many things she knew. She constantly heard messages of praise and encouragement from both parents, as well as recognition of her patience, love, and expertise. They would add: "You must be a born teacher. When you get to be a lady, you will teach thousands of children to learn many things." Those messages, according to D, ignited the desire in her soul to be a teacher.

> She constantly heard messages of praise and encouragement from both parents, as well as recognition of her patience, love, and expertise.

When she completed high school, she earned a scholarship to go to college. The family helped to provide funds for other expenses. Two brothers who were newspaper carriers used a portion of their income to help D purchase books. D also had a part-time job at college. She said that her education was a real family affair. This was true of the three degrees she earned; and those earned by her brothers and sisters.

D is now married with two children. She says that had it not been for those positive messages that kept unity in the family and positive mental attitudes, she would not hold the job as department chairperson at a college. These messages, according to her, are being replicated with her family.

MESSENGER E

As a successful farmer and landowner of hundreds of acres producing a variety of crops, timber, cattle, and poultry, E is known as an outstanding producer serving the needs of numerous consumers on a national level.

His positive messages were received from his tenant-farming parents, whose lifestyle was barren in terms of shelter, money, and necessary comforts for daily living. But, in the words of E, "there was a wealth of love, determination, support, and high expectations for me and my five brothers and sisters."

They often read aloud and encouraged him to read Matt. 17:20 in the Bible: "If you have faith as small as a mustard seed. . . . Nothing will be impossible for you" (NIV).

He said that his parents told him that one day if he worked hard and obeyed the Golden Rule, he would not be a tenant farmer but would be a landowner helping other people live better.

The future looked dim, according to E, but he believed what his parents told him. So he worked hard in school, helped with chores on the farm, and developed a love for farm life.

When he finished high school, he went to college on a scholarship, majored in agricultural science, and worked part-time in his department to supplement the scholarship.

When he graduated, he was hired as an assistant manager of a large plantation.

Living frugally, E said that he saved enough to buy a forty-acre farm with a dilapidated house on it. For many, he said, the house would have been considered beyond hope. He and his family found joy in working together during spare time making repairs and hiring contractors to do technical parts of the renovation such as electrical wiring. When it was completed his parents insisted on dedicating the house to God for the miracle that had been performed. Their son moved them from a four-room shack to a ten-room house that was good as new.

E resigned from his assistant manager's job and went into farming full-time. He continued investing in the purchase of more land and employed others, at a decent wage, to expand his crops.

His success came, according to E, not only because of his parents' words of faith in him, but because they often read aloud and encouraged him to read Matthew 17:20 in the Bible: "If you have faith as small as a mustard seed. . . . Nothing will be impossible for you" (NIV).

MESSENGER F

Messages came from F's grandmother, who became legal guardian of F and her sister when she was five and her sister was three. Their father moved to another city and never contacted them.

F's grandmother, a widow and domestic worker five days a week, took in washing and ironing nights and weekends to supplement her income. Yet, every day, according to F, her grandmother took time to read to them, played little games, and taught them how to do everything in the household.

She talked with their teachers and asked them to keep her informed of any of their needs. Being very religious, she took F and her sister to Sunday school and church every week. She constantly asked the pastor and members to pray that she would keep in good health to work and rear "her girls." She also asked them to pray that they would do their best to get a good education.

Both girls graduated from high school and received full scholarships to college. F became a registered nurse and her sister became a teacher.

F continued going to school while working and earned a doctor of philosophy degree. Now she has an executive position with the federal government. Her sister earned a master's degree and became a specialist in the field of reading.

They care for their ninety-year-old grandmother, who is still going to church every Sunday, has good health, and shares with many listeners frequently how God helped "her girls" become "great women."

F, often with tears in her eyes, says that she and her sister succeeded because of the love and encouragement they received from their only parent—a loving, caring, and concerned grandmother with positive messages for success.

MESSENGER G

Messages from G's father helped him and his two brothers succeed. G's mother died during childbirth of his youngest brother. His father, an elevator operator in an office building during the day, cleaned offices four hours in the evening and served as mother and father for the boys. Neighbors volunteered as caretakers of the boys while the father was at work.

By the time G was eight years old, he was helping his father with many household chores. Every day the father would give his sons positive reinforcement by sharing a message of faith: "We can show the world that we can succeed as a family by doing our best and make your mother, who is in heaven, know that you can become great men. Remember, she knows when you do your best and that keeps her happy." G said this message of doing his best for his deceased mother, his father, and for himself helped the brothers become goal-oriented.

When he finished high school, G went to work in a grocery store during the day and worked in a theater as a ticket collector in the evening. His younger brothers were in school, but carried morning and evening newspaper routes. Their father encouraged them to save part of their earnings. They had daily conference calls after the evening meal to discuss their day and to listen to their father sharing gems of wisdom about being the best citizens they could become.

> Every day the father would give his sons positive reinforcement by sharing a message of faith.

When G was nineteen, his father encouraged him and his brothers to pool their savings with him to open a small neighborhood grocery store. Working together, in five years' time, their monthly income had tripled. They increased the size of their store to a supermarket and hired people to help them operate it.

After the three sons married, their father decided to marry, too. Living in separate homes, they still have weekly conference calls and family meals with their father. Their positive messages of doing their best continue to give them reinforcement.

MESSENGER H

Overcoming a life of poverty in a low-income housing project with her divorced mother, H said that the positive message she remembered her mother saying was: "Now is not forever. If we work hard, you in school and I in my job as a factory worker, we can one day live in our own home."

H said this message helped her to study hard in school. She said that she checked out books and magazines in the library about homes and families, and often dreamed of living in a beautiful home with her mother. The more she heard her mother talk about their brighter future together, the harder H said she worked in school to help make it become a reality.

After high school, she went to a community college for two years and worked part-time in a library. After completing her course, she was employed by a major airline as a flight attendant.

And their dream of living in their own home came true. Not only did H and her mother have a beautiful home together, her mother took courses and became a real estate agent. Together they purchased several homes and they have visited many places with airline passes.

H said that positive messages of "now is not forever" made her know she could achieve the vision of living in a home, rather than in a crowded apartment in an undesirable and depressing area.

MESSENGER J

Messages from J's parents inspired her to succeed. She lived on a beach where her parents worked in a resort hotel. Life was very comfortable for J and her family.

A crisis came when she was eleven years old. Her father became ill with an incurable disease that caused him to become unemployed. Huge medical bills forced them to sell their lovely house and move to a smaller one in a substandard neighborhood.

J said that her father, in spite of his painful body-wasting disease, would tell her, "I love you and your mother. Promise me you will let nothing stop you from getting a good education." He would then say to her mother, "Remember, my dear, where there is a will, there is a way." Kissing him gently, his wife would raise his head to fluff his pillow. She would hug J with one arm and hold his hand with the other. Then she would reply, "Without you, it will not be easy; but with God's help we will make it."

> Her father, in spite of his painful body-wasting disease, would tell her, "I love you and your mother. Promise me you will let nothing stop you from getting a good education."

After the death of her father, J and her mother lived in poverty. At the age of sixteen, J said she became so despondent she asked her mother to let her drop out of school to get a job. Her mother tearfully reminded her of the promise she had made to her father to get an education. She told her again and again that developing mind power would help them overcome their economically deprived status.

J said she made many sacrifices to complete high school and go to college. With the help of a loan and a part-time job, she majored in business administration and earned extra money typing term papers for students.

After graduation, J got a civil service job and said she and her mother often rejoiced because of her father's message, which kept them going when times were tough and the road to success was crowded with obstacles. But that message, "where there is a will, there is a way," kept them climbing.

MESSENGER K

K's parents lived on a small farm and earned very little money from their corn and cotton crops. Many times they were unable to provide basic necessities for their family. Yet, her parents were happy because they would count their blessings of good health, a shelter over their heads, family, friends, and more, as they shared in family grace at meal time.

> It was a regular habit, K said, for her parents to think of others who were less fortunate than they were and help to fill their needs.

It was a regular habit, K said, for her parents to think of others who were less fortunate than they were and help to fill their needs. For example, they would share food with sick and shut-ins, and would run errands when needed. Whenever K complained about doing chores, her parents told her, "If you want to be successful, you must love your neighbor as you love yourself."

As K was finishing high school, she knew that her family was unable to send her to college. She planned to get a job and perhaps go to school at a later time. To her surprise, one of the elderly women she had been doing chores for through the years—a woman that everyone thought was a pauper—

Car Pool Auto Wash
9200 W. Broad St.
10:25am   6-03-08
WA:435018   SH 5311

Basic Wash   12.95
Tire Shine   5.00
Senior Disc   -1.50

TOTAL $:   16.45
Cash/Check   20.00
CHANGE: 3.55

"VISIT US ONLINE"
WWW.CARPOOL-LLC.COM

SEND YOUR QUESTIONS
OR COMMENTS TO
INFO@CARPOOL-LLC.COM

THANK YOU
Present this receipt
to Agent as your
**** CLAIM CHECK ****

informed her parents that she had sent money to the local college to pay K's tuition for four years.

Her parents' message that, "If you want to be successful, love your neighbors as you love yourself," became a reality for K. She said that as a professional interior decorator, a wife, and a mother, she is still practicing the message to help others as she was helped by her parents.

The messages of these ten persons are examples to inspire, challenge, and dream of ways in which parents, parents-to-be, guardians, and others who interact with children, in either professional or nonprofessional categories, may improve their performances as teachers and learners. May we be ever mindful that it is our task to help each child—little, big, or middlesize—know that he/she is someone special. Each person has possibilities within him/her to make this world a better place by the positive messages of hope, faith, and love given or demonstrated on a daily basis.

Telling is selling; showing is reinforcement;
but acting makes learning a reality.

Ten Commandments of Successful Parental Education Performance

Chapter 2

1. BE A GOOD ROLE MODEL AND ENGAGE IN TWO-WAY COMMUNICATION

Blessed are we to have the opportunity to observe dawning of new days, parading of seasons—Spring, Summer, Fall, and Winter—and to meditate with expressions of thanksgiving for life and its myriad opportunities to succeed. Equally as important is the opportunity to be a good role model for our future citizens—all children—to emulate our words, actions, and deeds. Unaware as we may be, the ways we talk, walk, speak, and communicate are moving pictures for young minds to duplicate what we portray.

Let us pause in our roles to bring others with us by talking and listening to children to determine their needs and interests. As we cue in on their needs and interests, we can help them in their tryouts for positive roles of success.

2. HAVE A POSITIVE AND TRUSTING MENTAL ATTITUDE

In order to help children climb the ladder of success, we must believe they can do it. The self-fulfilling prophecy is as great in parent-child relationships as in any career. Our attitudes will affect behavior, dreams, and aspirations of our children. We must trust them to think, plan, and make decisions at an early age. This will enable them to make greater decisions as they grow older. Trusting a young child to choose the color of socks he/she wants to buy or wear is an important beginning for him/her.

We must believe the fact that young children and others are capable of becoming "inner winners." Noted educational consultant, public speaker, advocate for children, and expert in positive thinking Reggie Smith declares that if one is not an "inner winner," he/she is an "outer doubter." As my teacher, he helped me to understand that "there are no born winners or losers, but born choosers." He contended that as human beings, we operate on one of four stages of beliefs:

- We are unwilling and unable

- We are unable but willing

- We are able but unwilling

- We are willing and able

The first three are negative and must be modified. With the help of caring, concerned, and committed parents and parenting-ones who have a sense of trust and a positive mental attitude, it is possible to enable children to become willing and able. When this happens, they can succeed in climbing the ladder of success that they choose as their goal.

The powerful effects of a trusting and positive mental attitude were imprinted in my mind by my grandmother who said: "If you can believe and have faith, you can look through muddy water and spy dry land; and you can take sour lemons in your life and make sweet lemonade."

Another strong lesson in trusting and positive mental attitude was shared by Napoleon Hill when he said: "Whatever the mind can conceive and believe, by the grace of God, it can achieve."[1]

Believe that children will have a sense of trust and positive mental attitude and communicate this belief to them. This will ensure their growth and development as successful, inner-winning personalities.

3. DISCIPLINE CHILDREN WITH LOVE AND RESPECT

Discipline, as used in this volume, means to teach children to be in control of themselves. This control must be part and parcel of all their actions. It does not mean making demands through punishment, but solving problems through positive actions.

Many times children act out their frustrations through destructive temper tantrums, fighting, yelling, and destroying belongings, etc. Behavior modification is needed to change these negative actions to positive forces. It can best be done through love and respect.

Parents and parenting-ones must help children gain inner control through positive, firm, and loving action. Care must be taken to reassure children that negative behavior is unacceptable, but that they are still loved.

> Care must be taken to reassure children that negative behavior is unacceptable, but that they are still loved. Discipline must be consistent and fair.

Discipline must be consistent and fair. It confuses children, young and old, to have an act accepted one time and then be punished for the same act at a different time. For example, a mother allows a child to turn somersaults in the living room when she is feeling well; but when she is suffering with a migraine headache, she punishes the child for annoying her with somersaults. Discipline, then, becomes a mixed signal for the child.

Because parents are human, it is to be expected that tolerance levels will fluctuate on a scale from one to ten, with one very negative and ten very positive. When parents or parenting-ones find themselves at five or below, they should explain to children why the behavior is not acceptable at this time. For example, if it is that they are not feeling well, they should tell children that their be-havior is making them feel worse and suggest that they engage in some quiet game. An explanation to children will help them understand why behavior once accepted is not tolerated at this time.

Basic needs that each child must have met are: (1) physical care, (2) protection, (3) love, (4) self-esteem, and (5) special interests.

When a child cooperates with parents or parenting-ones in obeying or granting a request, he/she should be given sincere, honest praise for showing respect and sharing love. This give and take of love with discipline enables the goal of self-control to be a positive force that can be reckoned with in teaching and learning.

A word of caution: Make rules simple and keep them few in number. Too many rules will result in chaos and confusion rather than produce peace and harmony—the primary ingredients of love and respect.

4. UNDERSTAND AND MEET UNIQUE NEEDS OF EACH CHILD

Just like fingerprints, there are no two children alike. This is even true in the case of identical twins. It is necessary, then, to give serious study through observation and communication to understand likes and dislikes of your children. Special consideration should be given to their strengths, weaknesses, successes, and failures in work and play, at home, school, and in community activities.

Basic needs that each child must have met are: (1) physical care, (2) protection, (3) love, (4) self-esteem, and (5) special interests. These are necessary for the following reasons:

Physical Care

Parents and parenting-ones should provide food, clothing, shelter, and health needs for children.

Protection

Safety of each child is a must for success. Parents should begin with infants to establish environments that are safe from danger. Adhere to common-sense practices, such as keeping matches, laundry bleaches, medicine, and other harmful materials out of the reach of children. Young children suffer in hospitals from home accidents that often could have been avoided if parents had provided necessary protection.

Love

Everyone, young and old, needs and deserves genuine love. Not only should children be told many times a day that they are loved, they should be shown through physical actions of kindnesses that they are truly loved. According to Reggie Smith in *The Best Course*, "It takes four hugs a day for survival, eight hugs a day for maintenance, and twelve hugs a day for success."[2] Since it takes three times as many hugs for success as for survival, parents and parenting-ones must find creative ways to give at least twelve verbal or nonverbal "hugs" a day.

Touching is most important when you are providing positive reinforcement to children. A pat on the shoulder; a gentle touch on the chin, nose, ear, or head; or a firm handshake reassures children that love is important and will be a sustaining force in the absence of parents.

Self-Esteem

Feeling good about one's self enhances feelings of success. Children must be helped to feel good about themselves. Avoid criticizing and complaining about deficiencies of children and build on their strengths by telling them they can succeed if they try. Giving verbal rewards for any sign of success will enhance self-esteem.

Special Interests

All children should be allowed to explore, experiment, and determine their special interests in hobbies and development of special talents. It is difficult for them to know and verbalize their interests until they are given many choices. Church, scouting, YWCA, YMCA, and other organizations enable children to become acquainted with many activities. The best organization, however, is the home. Parents can set the experimentation with varied interests. Through the use of inexpensive and salvage materials, many stimulating experiences can be realized. For example, musical instruments can be made from such items as cereal boxes, pots, pans, milk bottles, jars, etc. Flour and salt can be mixed together with water to provide play-dough for modeling. Old magazines and newspapers can be used for collages. Paper bags can be used for making masks. Shoe boxes can be stuffed with newspaper to make building blocks. Spools can be used for stringing beads or as wheels on a cardboard train, truck, or car. Scraps of fabric can be used for making designs, sewing, etc.

> Parents can set the experimentation with varied interests. Through the use of inexpensive and salvage materials, many stimulating experiences can be realized.

Taking children on walking tours around the neighborhood to see people working in various careers and talking with them about their occupations will spur interest in possible careers. Trips to libraries, museums, parks, zoos, etc., will also help stimulate special interests.

Pursuing special interests can be fun as well as fundamental in career development. Active involvement in the world of work for young and old will make special interests sparkle.

5. GIVE SINCERE, HONEST PRAISE LAVISHLY

Praise has the power to give children and adults faith in themselves to succeed in spite of obstacles they may encounter. Adults should find ways to give sincere, honest praise to children several times every day. Negative behavior can be changed to positive with praise when a little progress is made in the right direction. For example, when a child has the habit of slamming the door when he/she enters a room, adults should observe when he/she enters making less noise. Capitalize on this by saying: "I am proud of the improvement you are making by making less noise when you close the door." When a child puts away a toy after using it or cleans the room— praise, praise, praise.

Be good role models, and children will catch the spirit of praising by hearing you praise others as well as praising them.

Play a game involving all members of the family praising one another for success, small or great. Be good role models, and children will catch the spirit of praising by hearing you praise others as well as praising them.

6. BE PATIENT AND NONJUDGMENTAL

Patience is a virtue that many of us must continually work on to master. This is especially true when we work with our own children and other loved ones. When our children take too long to learn any skill or perform any task, it seems natural to criticize and pass judgment about why they are slow.

Sometimes we program them with negative vibrations with little statements such as:

- Why can't you do things like other children?

- What's wrong with you?

- You are slow as a snail!

The list of negative brands goes on and on.

Instead of being negative, program positive thoughts in the minds of children by saying: "You have not learned that yet; but with a little more practice I know you can do it!"

Avoid comparing children with others. Each has his or her built-in clock that determines how long it takes to learn, to know, to understand, and to process information. Being aware of this will enable you to have the "patience of Job" with children and the "persistence of the devil" in avoiding judgmental statements.

> Instead of being negative, program positive thoughts in the minds of children. . . . Avoid comparing children with others.

7. HAVE HIGH EXPECTATIONS IN A PARTNERSHIP OF TEACHING AND LEARNING

Expect the best from children and you get their best performance. Communicate to children your belief in their capability to succeed. Many studies have shown that the results of having higher expectations will yield high performance.

Program your children for success by sharing with them your observation of things they do well. Make them superstars for making progress, not only when they earn As or Bs in school, but when they increase production of any performance.

Let children know that you believe they can top their own record of achievement. Avoid having children compete with others. The best and healthiest achievement comes when a child competes with himself or herself.

Help children set realistic goals for themselves. Make a chart with them to record mastery of steps taken to achieve these goals. Remember that learning can be fun when thinking makes it so.

8. MAKE SACRIFICES TO SHARE HIGH QUALITY TIME AND LEARNING RESOURCES WITH CHILDREN

Research shows it is not the amount of time parents spend with their children that helps them succeed, but rather the quality of the time that is spent with them. A suggestion that seems to work for many children is to have them engaged with you for twenty minutes of undivided attention daily. This will be more beneficial than two hours of frustrated, distracted, or divided time.

Teaching children through activities will help them understand that we are both producers and consumers and it takes both for survival.

Spending time making a learning game together is more beneficial than going to a store and buying a child an expensive toy. Using time to find out what questions a child wants to ask you and taking turns asking him/her things about his/her daily activities will cement positive relationships and will help children become motivated to succeed.

Read to children daily and encourage them to read to you. Preschoolers can be encouraged to read picture books before they learn to decipher words.

Include your child in your career, assisting you in getting small jobs done whether you are a cook or a curator, or a doctor or a diesel operator. There are small tasks your child can learn to do, even if it is no more than opening doors for clients or handing you a needed tool. Teaching children through activities will help them understand that we are both producers and consumers and it takes both for survival.

9. EXPERIENCE JOY IN ACHIEVEMENT AND HUMOR IN DAILY LIVING WITH CHILDREN

Satisfaction should be experienced every day in the joy of doing some tasks well. Discuss with children what you did well and encourage them to do likewise.

Share jokes about your activities, even if the joke shows your imperfection as parents. Admit your mistakes and make a decision not to let it happen again.

Listen with your children to humorous people on television to observe how they make the world a brighter place with clean jokes and deep laughter. Read comic pages together with children to find humor in actions and words of characters. Discuss ways in which happiness may be found in work and play. Cultivate a sense of humor by reading or reciting nonsense rhymes, jokes, riddles, etc.

Practice making sad people merry by giving them something to laugh about. Help others smile by sharing your smiling face in meeting and greeting others.

At the close of each day, express gratitude for a joyful heart and encourage children to do the same. Then each day will continue to be lived to the fullest.

10. HAVE FAITH IN A SUPREME BEING AND CREATE AN ENVIRONMENT OF PEACE, BEAUTY, AND EMOTIONAL WELL-BEING

Faith in a power greater than self helps to strengthen personal faith. The Holy Scripture declares that if you have the faith of a mustard seed, then all things are possible. We must work to become actualized in our faith by developing a trusting relationship with children. Take daily walks with them to see the beauty of the universe. Discuss what you see, hear, and feel.

Provide a center in the home with beautiful pictures that may be made, cut out of magazines, purchased, drawn, or painted. Teach children to display their creations in an orderly fashion, for sharing with others.

Practice quiet time with your children for a short period every day. Encourage them to meditate by thinking of the things that make them happy. During a part of the quiet time, read beautiful poems and stories that portray peaceful scenes that bring inner peace and beauty in thoughts. Play soothing music and encourage children to talk about how it makes them feel. Ask children to share memories of beautiful

> Practice quiet time with your children for a short period every day. Encourage them to meditate by thinking of the things that make them happy.

places they have seen and to talk about places they dream of visiting. Help them understand that a vision of greatness with faith is a giant step towards success.

*Making a home run means
all bases must be touched.*

3 Milestones That Motivate Excellence in Parent-Child Relationships

Checkpoints help to make continuous assessments of who one is, what are one's goals, and the order of priority in which they will be achieved. Procedures to be used and designated dates should be established for achieving objectives. Brainstorming should be used to explore many methods of achieving objectives and deciding on the best possible procedure to use. Then one should step back and look at what else may be done to make maximum use of milestones that will lead to self-actualization.

Parents and children, out of necessity, must establish significant points that will lead toward excellence in teaching and learning. They need to clarify with one another at least four main checkpoints:

1. Establish what children need to learn.
2. Decide why they want to learn it.
3. Develop objectives and procedures for achieving goals.
4. Make a declaration of what else will be done to bring enrichment and fulfillment in their lives.

Here is an example of checkpoints in development of concepts, using apples to teach preschoolers:

1. The child needs to learn that an apple is a fruit and that there are several kinds of apples.
2. The child needs to know why apples are healthy and should be eaten instead of junk food.
3. Objectives for learning about apples should be established. These include identifications of apples from other fruits; recognizing different kinds of colors of apples; developing number concepts such as one-half of an apple, one-fourth, etc.; and expanding vocabulary with words associated with apples such as *fruit, peel, cut, slice, dice, apple jelly, juice, sauce, pie,* and *butter.*
4. Other activities that can enrich learning about apples may include taking young children to fruit markets to observe the various kinds of apples. You may purchase and prepare them to eat using a variety of recipes. Take trips to an orchard to see apple trees growing. Plant apple seeds. Together, make picture books of apples in various forms. Parents and children may read *Johnny Appleseed* and other stories about apples. They may create their own stories, poems, and songs about apples.

These checkpoints enable children and parents to learn, assess their learning, and to discover joy in experimentation and exploration of various avenues of research and evaluation of learning tasks.

*Establishing guidelines for success
in parent education is as important
as a blueprint is to an architect.*

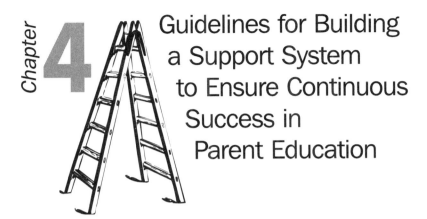

Guidelines for Building a Support System to Ensure Continuous Success in Parent Education

During the summer (more than twenty years ago), my granddaughter who lived in Detroit decided to spend her holiday from school with me in Virginia. This was a treat that I cherished. I considered how we would handle the daily working hours, since I was a twelve-month employee as an educational consultant in the local school system. It occurred to me to enroll the fourth grader in a creative program in an elementary school near my workplace.

Remembering that everyone would be a stranger to her in the school, I decided to build her self-esteem with positive reinforcement. I told her how fortunate she was to meet new teachers and students and to have fun in numerous creative activities.

In addition to our daily verbal communication on the way to and from school, I wrote several affirmations and put them in her lunch box. Samples of them are as follows:

Dear Kim:

Today, you are going to feel healthy, happy, and terrific in your new school because you will have a lot to share about your Detroit school. Remember: You can do all things through your Creator who strengthens you.

Dear Kim:
> Whatever your mind can conceive and believe, with the help of your Creator, you can achieve.

Dear Kim:
> Every day, in every way, you are getting better and better and better.

She never commented on the notes that I included with her lunch. However, one morning I forgot to write her a message. When I picked her up after school the first thing she said to me was: "Grandma, what happened? You did not have a note with my lunch today."

I apologized for neglecting to write a message for her and promised that I would be certain to include one every day. It made me happy to know she was reading them.

On the last day of her summer program, she was loaded with pictures and letters her teacher and classmates wrote to her expressing their gratitude for the information she shared about her school and places of interest in Detroit. After sharing them with me, she went upstairs and told me I could not come up there until she called me.

After about fifteen minutes she called me and said, "Grandma, come up here! There is some mail on your pillow for you."

Excited and surprised, I read my letter.

Dear Grandma:
> Thank you for sending me to that wonderful school. I love it, but most of all I loved the notes you put in my lunch box. I am going to share them with my parents and friends.
>
> > Love you,
> > Kim

Her message made me feel like I had climbed the ladder of success.

Parents and parenting-ones are a community of teachers and learners of the world's greatest possession—children. In building a support system for each other, they must make every effort to have oneness of purpose. They must recognize that where there is unity, there is strength. A strong support system is dependent upon each member of the team making a concerted effort to find needs and fill them.

A cohesive support group is necessary to reinforce and extend learnings about children. It takes a few interested parents or parenting-ones to form a structure of advocates for children. Extend invitations for others to join in making plans. Parents can then implement and evaluate those that will make a viable support system. This will ensure continuous progress in identification of problems and in finding the best possible solutions. In such an organization, where members are tuned in on the same continuum, the whole structure becomes stronger than the sum of individuals operating in a vacuum. For example, parents with similar interests in parent education can give extra support to one another by sharing knowledge, discussing role-playing skills learned, and applying knowledge to increase the number of supporters in the system.

Suggested ideas in planning, implementing, and evaluating a support system for continuous success in parent education performance are:

- Identify a group of interested parents and form a community of supporters.

- Share problems related to child-rearing practices and coping strategies for challenges related to child growth and development.
- Find human resources for assistance in solving identified problems. (Some sources are school personnel such as administrators, teachers, counselors, nurses, librarians, psychologists, nutritionists, etc.; child welfare agencies; parent-teacher association officers; and pediatricians, dentists, and other health officials, etc.)
- Organize subgroups to work on special phases of common problems.
- Set regular meeting dates for sharing progress reports with the total group.
- Read widely on topics of interest in parent education and involvement.
- Recruit volunteer specialists to conduct workshops for parent groups related to identified problems.
- Organize exchange clubs of books, toys, clothes, games, etc., that may be shared by members.
- Visualize success from high expectations set for the support system and make declarations of positive results.
- Disseminate knowledge, skills, and techniques to a wider audience of parents via newsletters, radio, and television. Communicate messages that will inspire others to join in an ongoing campaign for caring, sharing, assisting, protecting, and inspiring future citizens—children.
- Keep in mind that being a parent is the most important career an adult will ever have. It is a role that can be played only once in the lifetime of each child.

- Realize that it is difficult to correct mistakes in parenting because the scenes are not reversible.
- Do your best at all times and there will be no time left for regrets.

*Seeing is believing and
doing is the undisputed reality.*

Samples of Home-Learning Activities That Reach and Teach Learners

B ased on a format developed by Gordon and Associates for the federally funded Parent Education Follow Through Program (nationally validated for replication in 1977), the following ideas can be used by parents and parenting-ones. These concepts are "starter-uppers" to be extended, enriched, and personalized for reaching and teaching children.

Five basic sections—Title, Why, What, How, and What Else—guide planning, implementing, and evaluating ideas. Through the years, parents have found this format useful in thinking of fun ways to teach children at home. Teachers in many localities use this format in developing lesson plans that sparkle when ideas are developed to stimulate learning through the use of all senses.

Activity
ONE

Title: All About Me—The "Me" I See Is the "Me" I'll Be

Why: To elevate self-esteem and develop an awareness of self as a biological wonder.

What: Photographs and self-portraits, crayons, paper, pencil, mirror.

How: Show the child photographs of himself/herself. Talk about how special he/she is. Discuss the uniqueness of his/her picture. Point out the beauty of eyes, nose, face, and more. Discuss the expressions shown, such as happy, sad, excited, afraid, etc.

Encourage the child to draw a self-portrait after looking in the mirror to see the different body parts and physical features.

What Else: Have the child dictate or write a short story about himself/herself. Include such things as likes and dislikes; things that make him/her happy; and favorite foods, TV programs, books, toys, etc.

Use magazines to identify people in various careers. Ask the child to choose the one he/she wants to have as an adult and why he/she selected it.

Give the child sincere, honest praise for participating in the activity. Display his/her self-portrait and story where it can be shared with other family members.

Encourage the child to create pictures of himself/herself in the activities of the career he or she selected (for example: a doctor taking care of a patient).

Activity TWO

Title: My Family and Me

Why: To help the child know and understand roles of family members and to see how the division of labor makes work easier in the home.

What: Group or individual photographs of family members, pencil, paper, crayons, old magazines, scissors, and paste, glue, or tape.

How: Discuss each member of the family with child—name, occupation, relationship (brother, sister, grandparents), and how each one produces services and consumes services in the division of labor. Trace the family tree from great-grandparents to the present family. Indicate names, places lived, and occupations.

Use paper, pencil, and crayons to make a family tree that may be displayed in the home.

What Else: Use magazines to find pictures that represent members of the family. Cut these out and paste them in a booklet with the child's pictures. Identify occupations of people in pictures and show how these relate to family members in terms of similarities or differences.

Draw and color pictures of the family and write a story sharing the interdependence of family members as producers and consumers.

Ask the child questions about the family members that have more than one correct answer. Example: "What jobs are performed by Mother inside and outside the home?" or "How does baby sister help the family?"

Give the child opportunities to think about answers and encourage him/her to ask questions about family members.

Activity
THREE

Title: Workers Who Help My Family

Why: To make the child aware of the importance of community helpers in daily living; to determine the need for each helper; to develop observational skills; to become informed about jobs community helpers do to make family living easier; to learn about the tools each helper uses to get the job done; and to encourage the child to use creativity in expressing knowledge of community helpers.

What: Paper, pencil, crayons, scraps of material, paper bags, toilet-paper rolls, colored paper, scissors, paste, old socks, string, and other craft items.

How: Discuss the need for community people to help the family. With the child, make a list of helpers and activities they perform. Make a booklet of several sheets of paper.

Use a separate sheet for each helper. Each time a different worker comes to your house, have your child make an entry in the booklet. Example: The letter-carrier brings mail from near and far-away places. He/she needs a bag to hold the mail. The letter-carrier walks from door to door in the city or if houses are far apart, he/she rides in a special mail car or truck. Uniforms are usually worn, etc.

Be as descriptive as possible in discussing each helper such as garbage collectors; gas, electric, and water meter readers; paper carriers; carpenters; and plumbers.

Draw pictures and write a story about each one.

What Else: Help the child make puppets from the materials. A paper bag may be used as a base and decorated with scraps of material. A finger puppet can be made from a toilet-paper roll or a hand puppet from an old sock.

Activity
FOUR

Title: Map Skills and Fun Ways to Use Them

Why: To teach the child to understand the importance of maps as communication tools; that they are useful in many ways to people in various professions from transportation to science and technology; and that they assist in movement from place to place by indicating where places and things are and how they may be reached.

What: Paper, pencil, ruler, play dough

How: Discuss with your child four basic directions: East, West, North, and South. Have the child draw a rough map of his or her house indicating routes to take to find bedrooms, bathrooms, kitchen, etc. Have the child draw a map of the neighborhood. Show on the map landmarks such as stores, school, community centers, and church. Trace different routes that may be taken from his/her house to school. Determine which are the shortest and longest routes.

What Else: Read books about cartographers (map makers). Find out the preparation one must have to become a professional cartographer.

Do research to learn about the various kinds of maps and their uses, such as road maps, weather maps, and boundary maps of the city, state, nation, and world.

Encourage the child to use creativity in map-making by developing an imaginary city and using play dough to indicate places of interest such as government buildings, schools, banks, stores, houses, parks, and libraries.

Activity
FIVE

Title: Animal Categories and How They Help Us—Pets, Workers, Food, and Zoo

Why: To help the child learn names and functions of various animals and how they help us.

What: Magazines, dictionary, encyclopedias, scissors, newsprint, or other sheets of paper, pencil, crayons, and glue, paste, or tape.

How: Talk about the various animals in the home or neighborhood that are pets such as dogs, cats, fish, etc.

Visit a farm with your child to see animals at work such as mules, horses, donkeys, etc.

What Else: Visit the zoo and observe animals; learn their names, what they eat, where they are from, etc.

Visit the supermarket to see the various kinds of food—meat, milk, cheese—and the kinds of animals that provide each food.

Teach the child that there are four animal categories: mammals, insects, reptiles, and amphibians. Use the dictionary or encyclopedia to find exact definitions of each kind.

Go to the library and read books on different kinds of animals.

Play a game with your child naming as many insects as possible; also reptiles, mammals, and amphibians. Use a large sheet of paper folded into four parts. Label each section: (1) Insects, (2) Reptiles, (3) Mammals, (4) Amphibians.

Using magazines, cut pictures of different kinds of animals and paste them in the correct category. The dictionary or encyclopedia may be used to ensure accuracy. The child should be encouraged to draw the animals and learn to write their names if pictures cannot be found.

Activity SIX

Title: Trees—Helpers in Many Ways

Why: To teach children the names and uses of trees.

What: Trees in the neighborhood, books, paper, pencils, crayons, waxed paper, encyclopedias, newspaper, and glue, paste, or tape.

How: Take the child for a walk in the neighborhood or park to see trees. Identify the name of each tree and have the child collect a leaf from it. Wrap the leaf in waxed paper to protect it from curling and place it in a book to keep it flat. Clear contact paper may also be used to protect leaves.

Do research on each tree to find answers to these questions:

1. Does it bear fruit, nuts, etc.?
2. Is it used for lumber? If so,

what articles are usually made from it?

3. What medicinal use is made of its bark, roots, etc.?
4. Does it lose its leaves in winter? Why or why not?
5. Is it used for shade or decorative purposes?
6. What other uses are made of the tree?

What Else: Have the child look in the house and make a list of all things that came from trees. Examples: wood in the structure of the house, tables, chairs, beds, cabinets, paper, cardboard boxes, etc.

Go to the library with your child and find information on five trees that are not in your neighborhood. Describe their characteristics and uses.

Make papier-mâché trees with your child. Encourage him/her to draw or paint a forest of different kinds of trees. Encourage the child to invent imaginary uses of trees to help mankind.

Activity
SEVEN

Title: Famous People

Why: To help the child look for the best qualities in self and others.

What: Paper, pencil, pen, and a list of famous people that are favorites of your child. His or her name should be first on the list.

How: Talk with the child about ways in which people become famous, such as they do things well, are known as high achievers, or are distinguished for being excellent in a particular way.

Discuss special ways in which the child is famous. Example: He/she is unique. There is not one person like him/her. List the things he/she can do well (hobbies, talents, etc.). Think of other ways that make him/her famous.

Help your child make a list of favorite people he/she would

consider famous in one way or another. Write all of the positive things about each person on the list that could make each one famous.

What Else: Encourage your child to interview each person on his/her list of "Famous People." Prepare a list of questions to ask each one. They may be questions related to career, education, hobbies, or special talents.

Help your child make a "Who's Who" booklet and write the findings in each interview on separate pages. The booklet may be illustrated with a drawing of each person interviewed.

List the classifications of the careers of the people interviewed to see if the child's selection of famous people had any similarities or not.

Activity
EIGHT

Title: Food and Its Origin

Why: To study the interdependence of people by showing that it took many people to produce the food consumed in one day.

What: Menus for breakfast, lunch, and dinner; books; paper; pencil; and encyclopedia.

How: Help the child categorize the food eaten in one day such as breads and cereals, fruits, vegetables, meats, and milk products.

        List the careers of the people who provided services in the production of the food eaten. Example: The wheat farmer grew the wheat; the miller ground the wheat; the baker used products from the dairy farmer to bake the bread; the farmer raised animals that provided the meat; the butcher slaughtered the animals and helped to process the meat; inventors made scales to weigh the meat; transportation vehicles were used with operators to get the meat to supermarkets; it was packaged and priced by workers; salespersons sold it; and then a parent or parenting-one cooked it.

Encourage the child to take several other categories of food from its origin to the table and identify the kinds of workers who made them possible to be eaten.

Do research to find out where the food was produced, and the kind of climate and the processes used to prepare the food for consumption.

What Else: Find recipes in newspapers and cookbooks of different ways to prepare menus of the basic foods eaten.

Activity NINE

Title: Making Mathematics Fun

Why: To develop an awareness of the necessity of mathematical concepts in daily living and to show how knowledge of mathematics can be fun as well as fundamental for success.

What: Clock; meter stick, ruler, or yardstick; grocery store ads in newspapers; and a calculator.

How: Ask the child to prepare a log of time to get up, take a bath or shower, dress, eat breakfast, go to school, do homework, watch television, and play. Remind the child that this is using concepts of numbers to tell time.

Encourage the child to measure different objects in the home with both the yard and meter sticks. Let them compare measurements with each one.

Clock the distance from home to various places in miles and kilometers. Discuss how the numbers vary with each measurement.

Use grocery store ads and compare prices of food items in different stores. Use the calculator to see how much is saved by purchasing the same item at a cheaper price.

What Else: Give the child an imaginary $100 and ask him/her to shop for groceries to feed a family of four eating three well-balanced economical meals a day. Encourage the child to plan menus before shopping. Let the child use grocery ads to do the shopping, deducting the amount spent from the $100 after each purchase. Determine the number of meals that could be eaten.

Activity TEN

Title: Music—An Inspiration in Achieving Excellence

Why: To help a child develop good listening habits, understand stories involved in symphonies, heighten feelings of appreciation for beautiful melodies, and to relieve stress in daily living.

What: Recordings and tapes of symphonies, popular music, spirituals, etc.; books of biographies of composers and histories of compositions; and pictures of musical instruments.

How: Use the public library to check out recordings and tapes of various kinds of music and books on composers, musical instruments, and compositions.

Read and listen to music of a favorite composer daily. Then get acquainted with the music and life of others at the end of each month by playing a game to see how many musical compositions can be recognized without reading labels.

What Else: Play games with your child by humming melodies to see if he/she can recognize the song and identify an artist who composed or made it popular. Encourage the child to do the same with you.

Establish a music club with other parents and children. Take turns in conducting musical mini-workshops for the purpose of sharing, enjoying, and appreciating contributions of great musicians.

Encourage children to present talent shows to share their musical talents.

Activity ELEVEN

Title: Seeing the Beauty of the World through Art

Why: To train each learner to see that art is everywhere and to express messages of beauty, rhythm, and creation through exploration and experimentation with a variety of materials.

What: Paper bags, newspaper, newsprint, string, wire, tempera paints, brushes, cartons, leaves, paste, seeds, nuts, vegetables, fruits, shapes, everyday gadgets, and paper plates.

How: Take a walk around the neighborhood with a child to observe rhythm in lines, circles, and other shapes of objects you see. Observe different architecture in various kinds of buildings. Look at designs in leaves, rock formations, different shapes of shrubbery, nuts, seeds, and flowers.

What Else: Observe people to see uniqueness in physical characteristics. Watch animals to observe beauty in different body formations and movement during various activities.

Experiment with art materials in painting, drawing, and constructing favorite objects, persons, or animals observed.

Make prints using slices or halves of fruits and vegetables such as apples, green peppers, seeds; make handprints and footprints.

Do gadget painting with screws, bolts, and other household items. Dip them into paint and make designs on paper.

Make masks and puppets from paper bags, paper plates, and other objects.

Display the finished products and invite others to see the exhibit.

*An idea tested and found workable is
a precious gem that cannot be tarnished.*

Chapter 6
Tested Parent Education Ideas That Work

I n addition to developing a format for writing home-learning activities as a part of the model for the federally funded Parent Education Follow Through Program, Gordon and Associates suggested a set of teaching strategies. Ten "Desirable Teaching Behaviors" form the basic tenets for excellence in the teaching-learning process.

Since 1969, many professionals, paraprofessionals, and parents in numerous school systems throughout various states and in other countries have found these teaching strategies very effective. Learners at all levels can be helped to achieve maximum potential through the systematic use of these Desirable Teaching Behaviors. As a parent, grandparent, teacher of children and adults, supervisor, and educational consultant, it has been my pleasure to observe growth and development, both cognitively and affectively, with the use of these teaching strategies.

Comments from thousands of those utilizing these teaching-learning principles at home and at school state that they have been most helpful. There have been improvements in communication, self-esteem, and achievement in curricular and extracurricular activities.

In one-on-one interaction and in group settings, these behaviors are effective for enhancing excellence in interpersonal relations. I share them with the hope that every reader will find them fundamental for success in daily living and fun to use in helping oneself and others experience joy in teaching and learning:

1. Before starting an activity, explain what you are going to do.
2. Before starting an activity, give the learner time to familiarize himself/herself with the materials.
3. Ask questions that have more than one correct answer.
4. Ask questions that require multiple-word answers.
5. Encourage the learner to enlarge upon his/her answer.
6. Get the learner to ask questions.
7. Give the learner time to think about the problem; don't be too quick to help.
8. Get the learner to make judgments on the basis of evidence rather than by guessing.
9. Praise the learner when he/she does well or takes small steps in the right direction.
10. Let the learner know when his/her answer is wrong, but do so in a positive or neutral manner.

As planners of instructional activities, implementors of daily programs, and evaluators of progress of learners, you can use these Desirable Teaching Behaviors to serve as a guide for making the good practices in education better and the better practices the best. Success of any society is dependent upon enlightened citizenry. Therefore, when ideas are tested and proven to be effective educational tools, there is little or no need to reinvent substitutes.

Daily practice in the use of these Desirable Teaching Behaviors by members of a family, personnel in school settings, and during group interaction in community settings will make permanent patterns of behavior possible. Results from continuous use of these teaching strategies have increased faith in learners, established high expectations for performance, and increased genuine love for self and others.

Learners at all levels can be helped to achieve maximum potential through the systematic use of these Desirable Teaching Behaviors.

When all participants in the teaching–learning process engage in a cooperative venture in the use of Desirable Teaching Behaviors and a belief system that they will work, excellence in education will become a global affair. Enthusiasm for teaching and learning will become like a rippling stream. Its effects will be contagious to the ever-widening audience of interested citizens who deserve the best possible education that can be had.

The end is only the beginning
in the process of education.
The ladder of success must be
extended to eternity.

The Ladder of Success

is a challenge to climb.

Yet all things are possible with

caring, concern and confidence

with body, soul and mind.

Never give up and keep climbing

to achieve your goals!

—Epilogue—

This book was written to inspire, reinforce, and challenge each reader to know and understand that excellence in education is possible for every learner. When there is a positive mental attitude of high expectations by those who are teaching and those who are learning, whether they are adults or children, the self-fulfilling prophecy is at work. Each learner's theme song will be "*I can if you think I can.*"

As I look at parent education in the past and in the present, I firmly believe that parents and parenting-ones are the most effective teachers. They are first to modify behavior and they have about three times as long as professional teachers to make an impact on young minds. Whether this parent–child contact is favorable or unfavorable will affect attitudes and aspirations either positively or negatively. It is, therefore, necessary to give a concerted effort in making parent education/involvement first and foremost in the process of drawing out the best in children.

I believe the home should be the most important institution for reinforcing and enriching activities initiated in school. Knowledge of what is taught, why it is emphasized, and skills to develop understanding, comprehension, and application of what is learned, should be part and parcel of home/school activities with effective teachers in both institutions.

The abundance of salvage materials that are discarded in garbage pails can be used to make every home an exemplary learning center. For example, egg cartons may be used to teach mathematics, language arts, and creative arts. Labels from cans, cartons, and boxes may be used to teach comprehension skills in reading, mathematical concepts, colors, shapes, sizes, weight, and nutrition.

Climbing the Success Ladder: The Ten Commandments of Effective Parent Education Performance reinforces what parents and teachers already know. In some instances, it may serve to open doors to new understandings as excellence in education is enhanced.

The messages from those contributors to this book are reassurances that parents make the difference in helping children to overcome adversities and climb the ladder of success. With the support system provided by loving, caring, and committed parents, visions of success that may appear impossible will be actualized.

The Ten Commandments of Successful Parent Education Performance cited here are not ends in themselves, but serve as springboards for stimulation of sharing more ideas that may be disseminated. The same can be said about the guidelines for building a support system and samples of suggested home-learning activities. These are open-ended.

Readers are encouraged to share ideas that have worked. They will be reported in any follow-up publications to this edition with sincere thanks to each contributor.

While the contributors of the messages shared in this edition preferred to remain anonymous, it will be our pleasure to include names and brief biographical sketches in future publications. The format for submission of entries is on page 93.

It is my sincere desire that each reader will always operate on the continuum of "good," "better," and "best." Your goals and objectives for excellence will not stop with your good performance but will strive to make it better; and your better performance will stretch to your best.

—Feedback—

Report Messages of Success

(for recipients of parental support)

The Message: _____

_____

Why Was It Given? _____

_____

What Effects Did It Have on You? _____

_____

How Did You Use the Message? _____

_____

What Were the Results? _____

_____

Name: _____

Address: _____

Brief Biographical Sketch: _____

_____

Please forward your success stories to:

Dr. Virgie Binford

3027 Peabody Lane

Richmond, VA 23223

93

—Notes—

Prologue

1. Samuel J. Braun and Esther P. Edwards, *History and Theory of Early Childhood Education* (Worthington, Ohio: Charles A. Jones, 1972).

2. Sidney Cornelia Callahan, *Parenting: Principles and Politics of Parenthood* (Baltimore, Md.: Pengreen Books, Inc., 1974).

3. James Schiavone, *Help Your Child to Read Better* (Chicago, Ill.: Nelson–Hall, 1977), 5.

4. William F. Breivogel, et al."Training of Teachers, Parent Education Model," Final Report. Washington, D.C., U.S. Department of Health, Education, and Welfare (Oct. 1973), 5.

5. B. L. White and J. C. Watts, *Experiences and Environment,* vol. 1 (Englewood Cliffs, N.J.: Prentice-Hall, 1973).

6. John W. Warner, "Parents–Home Life: The Sinews That Bind Our Nation Together." *Congressional Record.* Washington, D.C., 125, no. 132 (3 Oct. 1979).

7. Ira J. Gordon, *Parent Involvement in Compensatory Education* (Urbana, Ill.: University of Illinois, 1970); Nancy Rutenber, *Parenting,* (Buffalo, New York: SUNY Press, 1979); and Richard L. Weinberg and Lynn Goetsch Weinberg, *Parent Prerogatives: How to Handle Teacher-Misbehaviors and Other School Disorders Problems* (Chicago, Ill.: Nelson–Hall, 1979).

8. Patricia P. Olmsted, et al. *Parent Education: The Contributions of Ira J. Gordon* (Washington, D.C.: Association of Early Childhood Education International,

1980), 3.

9.   Gerald Leinwand, *Public Education (American Issues)* (New York, N.Y.: The Philip Lief Group, 1992), 32.

10.   Ann Lloyd, *Tips and Tricks: Home Schooling Survival* (New Springfield, Ohio: Know More Publishing, 2001), 63.

11.   Larry Martz, *Making Schools Better* (New York, N.Y.: Times Books, 1992), 151.

12.   Ronald K. Pierce, *What Are We Trying To Teach Them Anyway? A Father's Focus on School Reform* (San Francisco, Calif.: ICS Press, 1993), 128.

13.   Jack Canfield, et al., *Chicken Soup for the Parent's Soul* (New York, N.Y.: Scholastic, Inc., 2000).

Chapter Two

1.   Clement Stone and Napoleon Hill. "Select, Prepare and Digest Your Food for Thought," *Success Unlimited* (May 1980): 8, 48.

2.   Reggie Smith, *The Best Course* (Richmond, Va.: University of Virginia Extension, 1985), 2.

—Bibliography—

Braun, Samuel J., and Esther P. Edwards. *History and Theory of Early Childhood Education.* Worthington, Ohio: Charles A. Jones, 1972.

Breivogel, William F., Gordon Greenwood, and Dorothy Sterling. "Training of Teachers, Parent Education Model," Final Report. Washington, D.C., U.S. Department of Health, Education, and Welfare, Oct. 1973.

Callahan, Sidney Cornelia. *Parenting: Principles and Politics of Parenthood.* Baltimore, Md.: Pengreen Books, Inc., 1974.

Canfield, Jack, Mark Victor Hansen, Kimberly Kirberger, and Raymond Aaron. *Chicken Soup for the Parent's Soul.* New York, N.Y.: Scholastic, Inc., 2000.

Gordon, Ira J. *Parent Involvement in Compensatory Education.* Urbana, Ill.: University of Illinois, 1970.

Leinwand, Gerald. *Public Education (American Issues).* New York, N.Y.: The Philip Lief Group, 1992.

Lloyd, Ann. *Tips and Tricks: Home Schooling Survival.* New Springfield, Ohio: Know More Publishing, 2001.

Martz, Larry. *Making Schools Better.* New York, N.Y.: Times Books, 1992.

Olmsted, Patricia P., Roberta I. Rubin, John H. True, and Dennis A. Revicki. *Parent Education: The Contributions of Ira J. Gordon.* Washington, D.C.: Association of Early Childhood Education International, 1980.

Pierce, Ronald K. *What Are We Trying To Teach Them Anyway? A Father's Focus on School Reform.* San Francisco, Calif.: ICS Press, 1993.

Rutenber, Nancy. *Parenting.* Buffalo, N.Y.: SUNY Press, 1979.

Schiavone, James. *Help Your Child to Read Better.* Chicago, Ill.: Nelson–Hall, 1977.

Smith, Reggie. *The Best Course*. Richmond, Va.: University of Virginia Extension, 1985.

Stone, Clement, and Napoleon Hill. "Select, Prepare and Digest Your Food for Thought." *Success Unlimited* (May 1980).

Warner, J. W. "Parents-Home Life: The Sinews That Bind Our Nation Together." Washington, D.C.: *Congressional Record* 125, no. 132 (3 Oct. 1979).

Weinberg, Richard L., and Lynn Goetsch Weinberg. *Parent Prerogatives: How to Handle Teacher-Misbehaviors and Other School Disorders Problems*. Chicago, Ill.: Nelson-Hall, 1979.

White, B. L., and J. C. Watts. *Experiences and Environment* (vol. 1), Englewood Cliffs, N.J.: Prentice-Hall, 1973.

—About the Author—

Virgie M. Binford is a graduate of Virginia State University where she earned her B.S. and M.S. degrees in elementary education. She specialized in early childhood education at Columbia University in New York City and earned her Doctor of Education degree in administration and supervision from V.P.I. and State University in Blacksburg, Virginia. She has furthered her education at the University of Virginia and in international studies in Africa, Asia, and Europe. She earned her Ph.D. degree from New Hope Bible Crusade College and Seminary in Baltimore, Maryland.

Her work experiences include thirty-seven years in the Richmond Public Schools as a teacher, supervisor, and director of various early childhood and elementary education programs. She served as adjunct faculty member in the School of Education at Virginia Union University from 1969 to 1987.

During the 1988–89 school year, she was employed by the Department of Education in the U.S. Virgin Islands, where she served as Federal Programs Monitor on the islands of St. Thomas, St. John, and St. Croix. Presently, she serves as adjunct faculty member at J. Sargeant Reynolds Community College in Richmond, Virginia.

Dr. Binford is actively involved in community service, where she shares time in civic, church, and educational organizations, and serves as a volunteer in several organizations. Some of the places where she finds needs and fills them as a volunteer are:

All Souls Presbyterian Church (Ordained Elder)
Alpha Kappa Alpha Sorority, Inc.
American Association of University Women

American Red Cross
Delver Woman's Club
NAACP (Life Member)
National Association of Phi Delta Kappa, Inc.
National Association of University Women
National Council of Negro Women (Life Member)
Phi Delta Kappa National Honor Society
Pi Lambda Theta National Honor Society in Education
Sacred Heart
Union–PSCE Advisory Board
Virginia Area Chapter of the National Coalition of 100
    Black Women, Inc.
Virginia Extension Service Advisory Board
Virginia State University Alumni Association
    (Life Member)
YWCA

SPECIAL AWARDS AND RECOGNITION

As a publisher of several books, public speaker, and volunteer, Dr. Binford has provided assistance for the needy in diverse areas. She has earned awards and recognition from a variety of agencies and organizations for providing exemplary services:

- The Educational Wing of the Juvenile Detention Home in Richmond, Virginia, is named the ***Virgie M. Binford Center for Education*** for her outstanding services in conducting workshops for youth who experience difficulty with coping in society.

- In July 2003, Dr. Binford received the **Distinguished Pi Lambda Thetan Award**. This

99

award is presented in recognition of outstanding contributions to Pi Lambda Theta and the profession of education. It is the highest honor Pi Lambda Theta can bestow on a member.

- Dr. Binford was honored in 2004 with the **Clara Barton Volunteer Leadership Honor Award**, the highest and most prestigious award an American Red Cross volunteer can receive.

- She also received the **Toastmasters International ATMS Award** in July 2004.